Life Cycle of a Pine Tree

by Meg Gaertner

FOCUS READERS.

PIONEER

www.focusreaders.com

Focus Readers is distributed by North Star Editions:
sales@northstareditions.com | 888-417-0195

Produced for Focus Readers by Red Line Editorial.

Photographs ©: Shutterstock Images, cover, 1, 21; iStockphoto, 4, 7, 8, 11, 13, 14, 17, 18

Library of Congress Cataloging-in-Publication Data
Names: Gaertner, Meg, author.
Title: Life cycle of a pine tree / by Meg Gaertner.
Description: Lake Elmo, MN : Focus Readers, [2022] | Series: Life
  cycles | Includes index. | Audience: Grades 2-3
Identifiers: LCCN 2021003739 (print) | LCCN 2021003740 (ebook) | ISBN
  9781644938300 (hardcover) | ISBN 9781644938768 (paperback) | ISBN
  9781644939222 (ebook) | ISBN 9781644939666 (pdf)
Subjects: LCSH: Pine--Life cycles--Juvenile literature.
Classification: LCC QK494.5.P66 G34 2022 (print) | LCC QK494.5.P66 (ebook) |
  DDC 585/.2--dc23
LC record available at https://lccn.loc.gov/2021003739
LC ebook record available at https://lccn.loc.gov/2021003740

Printed in the United States of America
Mankato, MN
082021

About the Author

Meg Gaertner enjoys reading, writing, dancing, and being outside. She lives in Minnesota.

Table of Contents

Chapter 1

Seed

The weather turns warm. The cones on a pine tree open. Seeds fall out. The seeds land on the ground.

Water might carry the seeds away. An animal might eat the seeds. The animal will get rid of the seeds when it poops. Seeds often travel a long way before growing.

Fun Fact

Some pine tree seeds have parts that look like wings. These seeds spin and float on the wind.

Chapter 2

From Sprout to Seedling

A seed lands in soil. The seed opens. A root grows underground. The root holds the seed in place. It also takes in **nutrients** from the soil.

A **sprout** grows up through the soil. It reaches sunlight. Then it is called a seedling. It grows needles. These are the seedling's leaves.

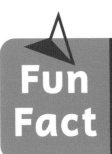

Fun Fact

Seeds might not grow right away. They wait until the soil and weather are just right.

Making Food

Like every plant, a pine tree makes its own food. The tree's needles take in sunlight. They also take in a gas from the air. The tree's roots take in water from the soil. The tree uses the sunlight's energy. It turns the gas and water into food.

Chapter 3

From Seedling to Sapling

Many things can hurt seedlings. Animals such as deer eat seedlings. Fire can burn seedlings. Too much water can also hurt seedlings.

But some seedlings live. They grow and become saplings. Saplings are several feet tall. Their **bark** is smooth. They can bend in the wind. But saplings are not **mature** yet. They cannot make cones. They cannot make seeds, either.

Chapter 4

Mature Tree

Mature pine trees have cones. There are **male** and **female** cones. Male cones make **pollen**. The wind lifts this powder up.

The wind carries pollen to the female cones. Over time, seeds form inside the female cones. These cones open. Their seeds fall. The life cycle continues.

Fun Fact

Female cones close to keep seeds safe. They protect seeds from the cold, the wind, and animals.

Life Cycle Stages

A mature tree grows pine cones.

A female pine cone releases seeds.

A sprout grows from a seed.

A sapling grows and grows.

A seedling starts forming needles.

FOCUS ON
Pine Tree
Life Cycles

Write your answers on a separate piece of paper.

1. Write a sentence describing how seeds are spread.

2. Which stage of the life cycle do you find most interesting? Why?

3. In which stage can a pine tree grow cones?
    A. seedling
    B. sapling
    C. mature tree

4. Why might seeds wait to start growing?
    A. They might spread pollen too soon.
    B. They might grow too many leaves.
    C. They might die if they grow in poor soil or cold weather.

Answer key on page 24.

Glossary

bark
The outer covering of a tree.

female
Able to have babies, make seeds, or lay eggs.

male
Unable to have babies, make seeds, or lay eggs.

mature
Fully grown.

nutrients
Things that people, animals, and plants need to stay healthy.

pollen
A powder from male parts of plants. It spreads to female parts of plants to make seeds.

sprout
An early form of a plant as it begins to grow from a seed.

To Learn More

BOOKS

Berne, Emma Carlson. *From Cone to Pine Tree.* Minneapolis: Lerner Publications, 2017.

Dunn, Mary R. *An Apple Tree's Life Cycle.* North Mankato, MN: Capstone Press, 2018.

NOTE TO EDUCATORS

Visit **www.focusreaders.com** to find lesson plans, activities, links, and other resources related to this title.

Index

Answer Key: **1.** Answers will vary; **2.** Answers will vary; **3.** C; **4.** C